M000167020

LIVING WITH
ISLAM

Other books by Brion Gysin include: *To Master a Long Goodnight*; *The Process*; *Brion Gysin Let the Mice In*; *Stories*; *The Last Museum*; and *Morocco Two*.

LIVING WITH ISLAM

Brion Gysin

Inkblot

Copyright © 2010 the Estate of Brion Gysin
All rights reserved
1st printing

ISBN 0 934301 50 6

Cover: Egypt Sunset circa 1923
Photo by L. Scortzis, Cairo
Cover design: hexit/mjk brooklyn, ny

Published by Inkblot Publications
Providence, Rhode Island

Distributed worldwide by Aftermath Books
Providence, Rhode Island
www.aftermathbooks.com

The publisher is deeply grateful for the assistance
provided by Dr Olaf Sorenseston and Raoul Duplatt, Esq.

Introduction

Brion Gysin was born in England in 1916 and spent the better part of his youth in Edmonton, Alberta, Canada before continuing his schooling in England when he was 16. Most of the '30s were spent in France and Greece, but included a trip to Algeria, perhaps his first taste of the world of Islam. He arrived in Morocco in the spring of 1950, at the invitation of Paul Bowles, after having spent the better part of 1949 in France and Spain, ostensibly researching the history of slavery, with funds from a Fulbright Grant. The grant was not renewed and Gysin was somewhat at loose ends. Jane Bowles, in fact, told Paul that she'd never seen Brion so desperate. And thus began Gysin's stay in Morocco, primarily Tangier, off and on for 23 years.

Bowles and Gysin did a fair amount of traveling throughout Morocco in 1950 and 1951. Gysin traveled the Sahara on his own for part of 1952. This manuscript was begun in 1952. It was revised and added to for a 10-year period, and probably finished in 1962. While he had visited Algeria in the late 1930s, I am convinced the majority of the info in this manuscript was from direct experience in the world of Islam, particularly in Morocco. Although Gysin had no training as a historian he was certainly a damn good one. And thus, his knowledge of Muslims and the history of Islam. One must remember Gysin did *not* become a Muslim. He felt *all* religion should be taxed out of existence.

The reader may question place names, spelling, and punctuation. I have changed nothing from the manuscript but for the occasional spelling discrepancy in Gysin's manuscript. Most readers will know of the changes in name of some of the countries included herein. The spelling, too, may have been unique to the time, and while Brion uses the American style of spelling for the most part, a number of British spellings do occur. While I was working with Brion on what came to be known as *Stories* (Inkblot, 1984) in 1984 he told me he would have used different punctuation than he had in the early 1950s. Yet he changed nothing in that particular book, most of which had been written in 1951. And thus I have changed virtually no punctuation in the present volume. I highly doubt the manuscript was submitted for publication.

Living with Islam is as valid today, or more so, than when it was written. The world of Islam is in the news daily. The supposed threat of Jihad is ever present.

Our copy of this manuscript was made from a copy owned by Am Here Books in 1983, when we copied what became *Stories* and *Morocco Two* (Inkblot,

1986). Shortly thereafter, all of the Gysin manuscripts in the possession of Am Here Books were sold to Raymond Danowski in England where they remained until 2004 when the collection was sent to Emory University in Atlanta.

Theo Green
Providence, Rhode Island
June 2010

Islam is an immense world which reaches all the way from Tangier to the Philippines. It is made up of over four hundred million Muslims of every color and all the races assimilated to the Arabs through the religion preached by Mohamed. Most Muslims like to think of themselves as Arabs for Arabic is the official language of their religion and law. Like the sands of the desert from which it sprang, Islam drifts over the ruins of all the foundered empires lying in fragments across North Africa, once Roman and Christian; Egypt, all of Asia Minor and Mesopotamia, across Iran to Afghanistan and Pakistan. It was transplanted into Malaysia and once flourished in parts of China as well as in various islands of the Indian Ocean and the Pacific. Islam still marches forward to this day across the savannas and on into the jungles of Black Africa.

This vast religious and cultural community has, for well over a thousand years, ordered the way of life of the warm countries which we have always considered remote, romantic and mysterious. These are the lands of caravans and oriental splendor contrasting with poverty and degradation; the lands of strange customs such as the veiling of women. The richly colored and even richly odiferous eastern scene when first viewed by many an American traveler seems to be only an insane confusion with decidedly sinister overtones. Today something new seems to be happening in the hitherto timeless and unchanging East which makes it imperative that we know something more about it.

As if in preparation for change, a good part of Islam has been dubbed The Middle East; a term which seems to have come out of World War II. Previously, people referred to the Near East, meaning in a broad sense, the Arab-speaking areas of the former Turkish Empire from Egypt to Iraq including Syria and the Arabian Peninsula. The

Middle East today is generally understood to include the predominantly Muslim countries from Morocco to Afghanistan; including Morocco, Algeria, Tunisia, Tripolitania, formerly Libya, Egypt, Israel, Jordan, Lebanon, Syria, 'Iraq, Saudi Arabia, the Yemen, Aden Protectorate, Oman, Kuwait, Bahrain, Iran and Afghanistan. Islam further includes Pakistan, the Sudan, Turkey, several provinces of Russia, Zanzibar and a good proportion of the population of Ceylon, Indonesia and the Philippines.

One can justify the term Middle perhaps because of the general latitude in which these countries lie, strategically between the richer and more popular subcontinents of China, India and Europe. In another sense, the organization called Islam has long served as a middle-man between the East and the West in both space and time. The Muslim populations have transshipped the goods and been a mercantile link for us with the riches of the Orient even long before Marco Polo passed through their jealously guarded monopoly barriers. Religious fanaticism and a hatred of the West which still exists to this day were originally stirred up to protect economic interests before Columbus discovered the sea route across the Atlantic. The effect of that would seem to have been so immediate that the Moors were expelled from Spain in the same year, 1492: the power of Islam was on the wane.

At the historic height of Muslim power Europe was utterly dependent on the Arabs. The last vestiges of the Roman Empire; its legal, economic and cultural organization of the West finally crumbled at the beginning of the 8th century in a terrible crisis brought on by the disappearance of gold. The Arabs had swept from Mekka to the Pyrenees in the time of Charlemagne and closed up the gates of Constantinople. The Christian Mediterranean was divided into two insecure basins surrounded by Islamic countries. The European Dark Ages had begun and the world gravitated

4

towards a newly founded city called Baghdad. It was toward that central point that the caravans of Asia slowly wound their way and there ended the great trade route which led to the Baltic, by way of the Volga.

Curiously, Europe owes its revival called the Renaissance not only to the fall of Constantinople to the Arabs in the 15th century but to the treasure of Greek knowledge, particularly the bases of mechanics and physics, which had been translated into Arabic when they had not survived in what was, after all, provincial Roman Europe. The Arabs and their converted Muslims in the countries of the Middle East had fallen heir to nearly 1500 years of Hellenist civilization which they spread as far west as their universities of Cordova and Seville. Both Oxford and the Sorbonne were offshoots of these great schools.

The culture of the Middle East is not only an intermediate unit between East and West but it is in many senses the ancestral area of both. From it we have received most of the plants and animals whose products we eat every day, the art of metallurgy, the alphabet with which we read and write and the religious way of life which regulates our behaviour. Naturally, to describe this civilization is an even more formidable task than to describe our own. In comparison our own is rather brief. The history of the Middle East goes back over at least five thousand years while ours is scarcely more ancient than the Roman period.

The social system of the Middle East has been essentially Islamic since the 7th century although it is made up of a mosaic of other cultural relics. The test of the strength of a social system is to submit it to strain and that of the Middle East today seems to be bursting at the seams. Is Islam, then, a still-growing force or a giant re-awakened by its twentieth century contact with the industrial West and newly strengthened by its fortuitous possession of vast oil reserves? Or is the Middle East simply the exotic door for a struggle which will tear Islam itself apart while its people can be persuaded to take sides for or against us?

It is impossible to look at any of the countries of the Middle East before understanding what Islam was and is. Essentially it is four things: it is a religion which, like Judaism and Christianity, is monotheistic – preaching only one God and claiming as its own all the prophets from Adam, Noah, Abraham, Isaiah, Moses and Jesus to Mohamed who is the crown of all the prophets and the last.

Secondly, it is a community of Muslim brothers and, therefore, a supra-national political unit much as Christendom was in the Middle Ages. In all conversation Muslims address each other as Brother; a term which they would never use in regard to a non-Muslim.

Thirdly, it is an extraordinarily conservative way of life which relegates the behaviour of the individual in stupefying detail; down to the manner in which fingernails may or may not be pared.

Lastly, it is an interpretation of history and a philosophical outlook more stringently narrow than our own has ever been at any time in our past. If the West may be said to believe that man was put here to work out his salvation, Islam believed that man was set on the earth to pray and, no matter what he may do about it, the final word lies with God.

The faith of Islam was first preached by a man named Mohamed who was born in Mekka, Arabia, about 570 A.D. He belonged to the prominent Hashimite family of the ancient and noble tribe of Quairaish. His grandfather had been the custodian of the Kaaba, a religious shrine then given to idolatry, which had been a place of pilgrimage probably since Stone Age times. Mohamed's family traced its descent from Abraham through his son

Ishmael whose mother was Hagar. The Jewish tribes of the same Semitic origin called themselves the sons of the same Abraham through his son Isaac. The Arab tribes were, thus, southern cousins who had never been through the tremendous group experiences of the captivities in Egypt and Babylon.

Mohamed is the only founder of a major religion whose life story is available to us in the full light of history. We have, however, no picture or statue of him because he expressly forbade all painting and sculpture as a part of his struggle against idolatry. Orphaned at an early age, he travelled with his uncle's caravans; married a wealthy widow named Khatija when he was twenty-five and she forty. Some fifteen years later, Mohamed began to have a series of spiritual experiences accompanied by revelations which, rather gradually, he and others came to accept as the voice of God speaking to him through the medium of Archangel Gabriel. As he gathered adepts and was consequently persecuted by his disapproving family and the townspeople of

Mekka, who feared to see their profitable pilgrim-trade disappear, he fled to Medina on June 20, 622 A.D. This flight was the Hegira and from it the Muslims begin their calendar.

Further revelations and a time of political struggle followed with Mohamed's party finally triumphant in all Arabia. At one point the Arab armies ventured north and came in contact with the forces of the tottering Roman Empire, ruled by the unsuspecting Emperor Heraclius from Constantinople. The prophet died in the year 632 A.D. at the age of 62 and, very shortly after his death, his inspired utterances were collected into a book known as the Coran.

Mohamed made no claim to being divine. He is *not* worshipped by his followers who are not called Mohamedans but Muslims, sometimes spelled Moslems. The Arabic plural is Muslimin, meaning those who submit themselves to the will of God. To become a Muslim it is sufficient to believe and say: "God is One and Mohamed is His prophet."

With the above simple formula, the original small band of fervent believers around the bed of the dying prophet had conquered half of the known world within living memory of the man who first uttered it. From that living memory of his spoken precepts, decisions, sayings and everyday acts, a second book was put together called the Hadiths or, collectively, the *Sunna*. The Sunna is the code of traditional behaviour and custom resembling English common law in that it is based on case histories and precedents. All orthodox Muslims follow this and are called Sunnites. No distinction was made between religious and civil law. An offense to the community of the faithful was to be considered an offense against God, the symbol of their mutual relationships.

Thus armed, the Muslims came quickly into possession of a part of the world which had been

Hellenized for fifteen centuries and was, in fact, the cradle of civilization itself. The converts to Islam brought with them the priceless heritage of antiquity which was soon translated into Arabic and through that medium handed on to us when perhaps all but Aristotle would have been lost in our medieval Dark Ages.

Mohamed may have intended to be a reformer rather than the founder of a new religion and the original flexibility inherent in such a position greatly aided the Muslims as the creators of a new super-state. The followers of the two older religions, Judaism and Christianity, were recognized as "People of the Book"; the Old and New Testament with which the Coran has so many points of resemblance. All other peoples were Kaffirs or heathen; people beyond the pale for whom conversion was, nevertheless, made easy. The Jews were denounced for their particularism and the claim that Jehovah was their God alone and had chosen them for their refusal to recognize Jesus and Mohamed as prophets; the Christians because they worship Jesus as divine and because of the doctrine of the Trinity.

For Muslims, God is "closer to a man than the vein of his neck," and, at the same time, beyond all human knowledge; Unnamed and Unnamable. The word Allah is merely a useful approximation of His Unknown Name to be called at least five times a day at the indicated hours of ritual prayer at which a Muslim must turn to Him, pure in heart and ritually clean in body, facing towards Mekka.

The five Pillars of Islam are: the Profession of Faith, Prayer, Almsgiving, Fasting and the Pilgrimage to Mekka.

The Profession of Faith, as previously mentioned, is sufficient to make anyone a Muslim if said with intention at a critical moment; with a sword at one's throat for example.

The Muslim prayers are to be said five times a day: at dawn, noon, mid-afternoon, sunset and dusk. The devotee must be ritually clean and Muslims pay great attention to bathing. In the waterless desert it is permitted to "wash" with sand. The prayer is performed rather than merely said, for a complicated gymnastic ritual of bowing and prosternation is an integral part of it. In practice, many city-dwellers no longer say all their prayers and it is hard to imagine how they could if they work in a factory, for example. Prayers may be said in public or in private when the musical call sounds from the top of a mosque. The noonday prayer on Friday is the most important and as obligatory as Sunday church-going is for Christians. Friday has only recently become a day of rest and closed shops, however, as if in imitation of or protest over Sunday closing by Christian firms in Muslim countries. Women do not attend the mosque except in a little latticed corner reserved for their observation. They pray in private without the ritual of prosternation which is obligatory for men.

Almsgiving as an article of faith was devised as a sort of income tax graduated so as to fall more heavily on the rich than on the poor and is calculated yearly on negotiable property free from debt. The alms must be given personally to the poor. There is also an organization called the *Habous* to which a man may leave his property. The *Habous* provides for the upkeep of mosques, schools, orphanages, cemeteries and charitable institutions. It also administers the estates of minors like the old English Court of Chancery. Charity is not an institutional affair in Islam for the faithful are enjoined to give directly to the poor: a beggar is never spurned nor despised. To some extent begging is considered a perfectly honorable profession: a beggar is God's object lesson to us all, pointing up our own blessings and the fragility of man's fate.

The last Pillar is the pilgrimage called the Hadj which every Muslim is enjoined to perform in his lifetime. To have accomplished it gives a man the right to the title of Hadji and usually brings to an end the various deviations such as frequenting Christians, smoking and drinking which he may have practiced in his guilty but carefree youth. It takes place in a special month, the twelfth of the Muslim lunar calendar, and brings together the faithful in Mekka where none but the faithful may enter to perform certain rites some of which are much older than Islam. Perhaps the most important role of the pilgrimage is the reiteration of the fundamental unity of Islam and it brings the far-flung Muslims into contact. It is also a very big business.

Islam is certainly unique as a religious organization inasmuch as there is no clergy. Any pious and learned man may officiate at the prayer in the mosque and thus be an *imam*. As Islam is, however, both the state and the religion at the same time the officials of the state, sultans and judges, might be said to correspond to the hierarchy of other religions. All law and suitable knowledge is held to be found in or to flow from the Coran. The Coran may be read through in a single night and is known by heart to the majority of the literate and to many Muslims who repeat it parrot-fashion or chant it without understanding the words of a language as antique as Church Latin. All Muslim schooling is the learning of the Coran by rote and higher education is the commentary texts of the same book.

As all Muslim society rests on the five Pillars, the Coran and the tradition of the Sunna, it is to be wondered if they could bear the superstructure of a modern industrialist state.

The Coran is superb poetry; held to be almost impossible to translate. Any Westerner who attempts it will agree with this opinion. In it the path of virtue is bordered by oriental flowers of rhetoric and leads to the admirable if startling proposition that: "The ink of the scholar is more holy than the blood of the martyr." Prayer, submission to the will of God and the pursuit of knowledge are held to be the compatible cornerstones of life. The path of virtue is held to be smooth, pleasant and there is no preaching of hell-fire. Most Muslim doctors of religion hold that Allah in His mercy would not permit Gehenna to exist for all time.

The Ten Commandments with their lapidary "Thou Shalt nots…" find no exact counterpart in the Coran, yet practically all the same virtues are approved and the same vices condemned as in the other "Religions of the Book." Emphasis may seem to vary considerably. Sexual repression is unknown in Muslim society: there is no echo of Saint Paul. The Coran does not preach asceticism, nor celibacy nor the monastic way of life. Islam is a practical religion that has always been suspicious of even its own mystical movements, known as *Sufism.* It preaches, rather, the virtues of moderation; underlines the sanctity of hospitality and the equality of all. The whole social structure, even as reflected in its uniformity of dress, is so essentially democratic that it is virtually impossible to tell a prince from a pauper. Visible outward equality is said to be the social reason for the veiling of women. There is no aristocracy but that of the *Shorfa* (sing.: sherif), the descendants of the Prophet.

Islam as a political community has the advantage of a common language much as Christendom once had Latin. In actual fact, the Arabic spoken in the street differs as much from one country to the next much as Cockney does from Brooklynese but educated people can understand each other with little trouble. All Muslims call themselves brother and are fundamentally united against the rest of the world. When reproached with particularism they may shrug and say: "Why don't you become a Muslim, then? All you have to say is the profession of Faith and we'll talk." This same particularism has a famous name which has an ugly ring in our ears: *Jihad*, the Holy War.

The Coran proclaims: "Kill the Infidel wherever ye shall find him." It is true that it adds somewhere else: "Do not rush into a *Jihad* lightly"; the part of prudence. As in other Holy Books, one can find a text to suit one's need of the moment but it must be realized that Islam is essentially a war-like religion as is any structure of opinions which is authoritarian. One language and one law from end to end of the structure once could raise Islam like a lever beneath a single block. It would be foolish to claim that such an absolute unity or uniformity of interests exists throughout Islam today.

There has been, almost from the very beginning of Islamic expansion, one great schism which might be likened to the rift between the Roman and the Greek Orthodox churches of Christendom. What has never taken place within Islam is a movement corresponding to the Reformation. Is it not possible that this "Reformation" is what is about to take place under our eyes today? Nationalist movements and the burning desire to possess what the West has achieved have brought many new leaders to understand that the first step towards modernization is to secularize the state. According to the Coran, however, there is only one law. Partly thanks to our Roman heritage the West has grown up with three codes: civil law, criminal law and canon law. Islam only foresaw a theocratic state.

This basic problem was first presented in modern times by the example of the Turkish nationalist revolution. It should not be forgotten that this movement, along with Arab nationalism in Arabia, was put into action by potent agencies intent on winning World War I. Much has been done since by still more potent agencies intent on winning World War II. These agencies are, of course, still at work.

It is, therefore, not the Coran nor a religious revival which is likely to bring about changes in

Islam. It is, rather the ideas of the French and Russian revolutions and the expansion of mechanized society. Peasants with a pattern of life established and adhered to for thousands of years have been attracted to the newly grown cities and put to work in factories established by Western capital. Little wonder that personal morality, which was all of a piece with tribal morality, has been shattered when the original pattern was broken. The Muslim with whom one is most likely to come in contact is a man dispossessed of his heritage, liable to be unstable, touchy and resentful; possibly a dangerous element in a crowd.

In each Muslim country there is an internal struggle between what might be called the Old party and the New. Both agree on one thing: their opposition to the West. The leaders of the New parties are generally at least partially Western trained.

The one section of Islam which has hardly begun to move is the one which must surely bring about the most radical change in the whole structure: the women. No one speaks of them and questions relating to them scarcely appear on the programmes of either the Old or the New parties. Given the lesson of what has happened to our own society in the last fifty years it must be assumed that they will eventually speak for themselves.

What is the position of women in Islam? It would seem superfluous to point out that any social reform can have little effect while they, be they happy or unhappy, live neolithic lives in the shadowy background of the family cave as it were. In the Arab world the family is a complex unit comprising several generations and is comparatively self-sufficient. It is unusual to have intimate friends who are not relatives. It is, therefore, neither fitting nor really necessary that women should go out of their homes. The highest boast that a young man can make about his still unseen bride-to-be or that a father or brother can make about a marriageable girl of his household is, "She has never seen the street." It is likely to be literally true only in a well-to-do family whose town-house is really more like a small village with its own gardens and baths. The terraces and flat roofs of all houses are reserved exclusively for the use of the women. No adult male of the household may appear on them until after dark. When a woman goes out she does so accompanied by female servants and relatives and she is veiled.

The veiling of women is not a religious precept but a social custom. It is, therefore, something which could and may disappear very rapidly. The consequences will be considerable. It is generally considered that the Sultan of Morocco at one time very nearly lost the regard of his people because he allowed one of his daughters to be photographed in a bathing suit. It is almost certainly true that the King of Iraq was so appalled when he met these young ladies that he refused to consider an alliance with a family so "advanced". It is a fact that Muslim young ladies who wear bikinis on the Riviera put on veils when they return to their own countries.

Veils are never worn inside a house; therefore, the entry of a strange, unrelated male requires domestic readjustment and the retreat of all females into nether regions from which they may emerge only when the guest departs. It is easy to see why there is only the most formal and absolutely imperative hospitality offered within an Arab house. Visiting foreign women on such unusual occasions assume the rank of "honorary men," are entertained with them and may be sent for a side-visit into the women's quarters. They may emerge with varying opinions as to the status of Muslim women. If they have the occasion to study the situation they will probably end with the idea that Muslim women are quite as clever as any other women and have ways of their own for making the best of any situation. There can be no doubt at all, however, that education is a vital necessity. With the advent of radio and television everything should be possible; unfortunately little or nothing has been done to use either to any real purpose. In countries dominated by the French or the English the answer has always been that a solemn promise had been given to respect all religious prejudices. Nothing can be done except by the Muslims themselves.

During the hectic days when Morocco hailed the return from exile of the Sultan and celebrated its independence, a number of young women took advantage of the general excitement to rush about without veils. They were usually hooted or threatened and even manhandled by the male population. During the present war in Algeria there are female nurses on the rebel side dressed in smart Egyptian WAC uniforms. They are said to have been recruited from the "entertainment" world. In the Algerian cities a number of women haven gone unveiled in recent years but such emancipation is at present considered rather suspect as a sign of sympathy with French ways. In independent Tunis the situation is similar. In Tripolitania there are new mixed schools for the elementary grades which are viewed with alarm by the older generation. In Egypt, Mrs Doria Shafik, the head of the suffragette movement, has been jailed as anti-Nasser. Syria and Lebanon are a mosaic of Muslim and non-Muslim communities: the veil is worn as a badge. Kemal Ataturk forbade the wearing of the veil by law in Turkey more than thirty years ago but ladies are still inclined to stay at home. In the countries of the Arabian oil-rich Peninsula most women are not only heavily veiled but forced to tie on a tight mask which is worn even about the house or camp and removed only at night.

With all these and other variations of the status of Muslim women, such as the fact that country women of Berber origin in Morocco do not veil at all; it is essential to bear in mind that the sequestration of women is at the very heart of Muslim civilization. Any change would affect the entire social fabric of their world. Even the physical details of their lives have been shaped that way for over a thousand years.

Every Muslim house is built to afford the women their seclusion. The Arab house turns in on itself with no exterior windows that are not hooded and latticed. The single street door gives into a blind dog's-leg passage so that no passer-by can glance inside. Only members of a family enter and a stranger is introduced only after preliminary warning has been given to the womenfolk to hide themselves. The terraces belong to the women; men live in the streets and the cafes are their clubs.

Within, the Arab family lives as though a house were merely a tent of stone and mortar. There is little furniture other than cushions, mats, rugs and hangings. One has the precarious feeling that everything could be bundled up, loaded onto the back of a donkey or a camel and carried away in an hour even though the family may have been living in the same house for generations. Rooms, as beautiful and agreeable as they may be, have no particular designation. People sleep anywhere, often in their clothes. This hardly matters in the case of flowing Arab robes but it helps to explain why Muslims usually look a little rumpled when they take to Western style suits. There are no closets but lots of chests. There is no dining room: one may eat anywhere they fancy or the weather bids and every meal is as delightful as a picnic. Men eat together and eat first; women eat together later. The master of the house often eats quite alone and may prepare his own meal or have his own male cook for fear the women might decide to put potions in his food. There is no kitchen as a rule. Women cook over pots of charcoal: one day in the patio, another on the stairs; tomorrow on the flat roof terrace. The cuisine is often exquisite and varied but the service is delightfully simple. Hands are washed at a basin and ewer at the table and Muslims eat with their right hand only. There is usually only one plate to wash and no silverware. Thus, even in a palace, domestic arrangements are of a nomadic gypsy simplicity. Add slaves and servants to this picture and one realizes that the women have almost nothing to do but prettify themselves, think and talk about men when they are young or intrigue and fight with the other women. In other words, half the manpower of the entire society stands idle and degenerates. No woman, however, remains unmarried: old maids are unknown in Islam.

Polygamy and easy divorce make women an expendable commodity to which little value is given. On the other hand, the veil and the closed character of the houses make anonymity comparatively easy and secure. Women simply gather up a bundle, preferably of money, and disappear except from the most closely guarded houses. Wild and dangerous intrigues are the rule rather than the exception. As men expect nothing but deception from women they are paid in their own coin. As women are not allowed out, female peddlers, beauticians, midwives or just plain go-betweens circulate through the harem world. It is said, quite believably, that a daring, insistent and well-heeled lover, a Muslim Don Juan, can make contact with any woman in Islam from the sultana on down. Women have so little to lose, perhaps, that they enter whole-heartedly into the most risky intrigues with no thought of the consequences. They are vital, fierce, fiery, reckless, swift in their passions until age and a hard life stifles their flame.

Very young marriages are the rule in the country, as in other societies for that matter; thirteen is not considered too young. In the cities, on the other hand, girls are married from eighteen to twenty four or so but a woman is old at thirty and often a hag at forty. Once divorced, a woman may lead a very free life indeed and marry many times again. Marriage is a contract, not a sacrament, and may be dissolved considerably more easily by the man than by the woman although her family can usually bring pressure to bear for a divorce by mutual consent if they are willing to pay back to her husband the bride price.

There are no literate women and few enough literate men. There is no intellectual life at all for women. There is no theatre and the movies are a rare and highly supervised treat. They have at times been forbidden altogether to women as most recently by the nationalists in Morocco. Banners over the market place in Tangier recently proclaimed that it was a jail offense for both the man and the woman who walked side by side in the street. Good women are simply not supposed to go out except to their own marriage or to their own funeral. Weddings, for example, are two quite separate festivities; one revolving around the bride and the other around the bridegroom. The party is over on the third day when the two principal parties have finally met and consummated their marriage. The proof of the bride's virginity is shown to the guests who toss wedding presents of money into the sheet and depart. Mixed company is a very private business in Islam. All Hollywood to the contrary, women do not dance in front of men unless they are practising the oldest profession. They are called *shaikats* in Morocco, if they know how to sing and dance, and they are now supposed to have been abolished by the new nationalists. Women's lives in Islam are, by any Western standard, almost sub-human.

Aside from all other considerations, it must be admitted that with half the population veiled and uneducated, the principal characteristic of all Muslim countries is the predominance of the underprivileged. Add to this the fact that these are all essentially agricultural economies tilling poor soil with insufficient capital and, one might say, a unique psychological approach which derives directly from the philosophy of their religion which is, at the same time, both the outer and inner aspect of their social organization.

For example: the vast irrigation systems of Mesopotamia were inherited from the Iranians and even copied with success in Muslim Spain where they work to this day. In the Middle East they were wrecked by the hordes of Genghis Kahn and they have never been repaired. Vast areas reverted to desert. North Africa was called the granary of Rome: not another bushel was exported until the French took over. All Roman marbles in the noble cities which stretched from Tangier to Alexandria were burnt for lime by the Arabs. Their own historian of the 14th century, Ibn Khaldoun, says that the Arab is a man who would knock down a temple to have a stone against which to set his pot over the evening fire. He also stated that one could still travel from Tangier to Tunis in the shade of ancient trees. When the French landed in Algeria in 1830 they found a desert almost down to the sea. One hundred years later vast areas were reclaimed and under cultivation or reforested on soil literally recreated by European direction and labor. Today a huge proportion of that has been laid waste again and the new forests flame daily to no particular purpose other than to inspire terror.

Generalizations are said to be dangerous but Muslim society is more authoritarian than even Puritan communities aspired to be. It has stood solid as a block for well over a thousand years and today, still, it steeps 400,000,000 lives in an all but identical moral climate from the Atlantic coast of Africa to the islands of the Pacific. The pervasive environment produces no adolescent rebels as ours does except where Western schools have had their influence. The culture in which Muslims lead their lives from birth to death is as different as possible from the air of Christendom which we all breathe no matter what our religious denomination or lack of it. If we travel the length and breadth of the Americas and know all the countries of Europe as well as we know the forty-eight states, we still know only one thing: Christendom in its internal diversity.

If we are to get to know something about these strange, overwhelmingly numerous and newly powerful world-neighbors, the Muslims of Islam, we might begin in almost any country of the Middle East which is available for travel but it will do no harm at all to bear the following generalizations in mind.

In Islam a Muslim thinks more or less thus:

Man is put on earth to fulfill the will of Allah and not to work out his own destiny. The purpose of life is prayer rather than work. Property of fellow Muslims is, theoretically at least, sacred. *Only* Muslims have property rights and all Westerners or others present who do not become Muslims are mere trespassers in Islam. Logic is purely a Western concept. It is not a rule of the universe and it would be absurd (even illogical) to demand it of Muslims. The concept of duty to one's fellow man is also a Western Christian concept. Muslims know only fellow Muslims. Every man is an island. Every Muslim is a solitary adventurer, gambling his life in a world-game where he knows the odds are against him. He has nothing to lose but his life and that belongs to Allah, anyway. A man's life is a mere bubble in an endless sea. Time is of almost no importance. Muslims do not have birth certificates nor keep track of their ages. One is a child, a man, a graybeard and one dies. When that happens there is a moment of solemnity but little mourning.

In the Muslim world, all social activities and particularly the relationship between the sexes is out and out lifemanship. Love is violent desire; sex an act of aggression which must be paid for by the person who desires. Self-control is not a virtue and in no way admirable. In a Christian it is considered to be a sign of cowardice. Lying is not only the breath of life but the essence of politeness. It is rude and ill-mannered, not to say insanely dangerous, to say what is in one's mind. A lie is always and in all circumstances preferable to the truth.

It is sinful to fear or to try to foresee the results of one's own actions. To fear any part of life or to fear death is to fly in the face of God's Providence.

To be prudent, frugal or provident is sinful for it implies a distrust of God's Mercy. Banking is a sin expressly forbidden by the Coran. Gratitude is absurd and even sinful: everything comes from Allah and the giver is merely an instrument of Allah. He who receives is blessed for it shows that this is in the good graces of Allah. Non-Muslims are sent along by Allah to be plucked.

Lest all the above may seem too appalling, it must be added that the Muslim way of life fosters certain virtues to an extraordinary degree. Hospitality and generosity cannot be exaggerated and, for them, may often be ruinous. The poorest man acts like a *grand seigneur* with the things of this world. One should be careful about what one accepts; if only because it would be uncomfortable to realize that one had just ruined one's host. This may quite easily happen in any country of the Middle East. There are two basic principles behind this. First: what Allah gives, Allah may also take away. It is, therefore, better to profit from it while you have it and He may give again. Secondly: what is mine is only a loan from Allah and is, consequently, yours. It follows that what is yours is mine and I fully expect you to give it to me if I should ask for it or appear to need it. There is a consequent disregard for property-values which can make a Westerner quite nervous.

Unencumbered as they are by so many of our preconceived ideas, Muslims seem to enter directly into the essence of life like fish in a clear stream. Like fish, they may seem at times to be oddly undifferentiated. For example, an astounding proportion of all males are called Mohamed and several brothers may be given simple variants of that same name, such as Hamid, Hamidou etc. They very rarely have a family name. One is simply Hamid son of Hamid of such and such a place. In a nomad camp or even in a large city, the various households seem, each one, to be only another living cell in a hive through which pulses, strong and even, the life of the whole community of Islam from end to end. It is, admittedly, curious that one who would hate to live in a Levittown should love life in the Casbah. Yet, the former seems all a-jangle with machine-living and internal conflict while in the other one shares the peace of mind of the Muslims.

For that Muslim peace of mind, which can be so real a thing it seems to hang like a pearly veil over the white cubes of an Arab city or be the very air one breathes in the desert, they pay what we may well consider a high price in creature comforts. At the same time they are more directly sensual than we. They are at all times intensely aware of their senses through which they receive extraordinarily limpid primary impressions with an immediacy which we can find disconcerting. They expect to satisfy their senses with a candour that we cannot allow ourselves. For them nature commands and man obeys with his body. If they have little or no forethought, they have no bitter afterthoughts. What we call repression is virtually unknown to them. It would be impossible to imagine a Muslim going to a psychoanalyst. Insanity does exist and is treated with a gentle tolerance verging on awe as if, by the blackout of intelligence, a madman entered more directly into contact with the overwhelming force of Allah.

A Muslim neither fears nor loves Allah; he simply knows that man exists in relation to His inexorable might. Man must live with patience and faith. No matter how things have turned out, that is the way they *must* turn out because that is the way they *did* turn out. It is useless to complain: what happens happens. This is the simplest exposition possible of the well-known "Kismet" or "Mektoub". The conditional does not exist in the Arabic language. If a misguided Westerner should ask a Muslim: "If you had done that sooner what would have happened?" the Muslim answers patiently: "But I did it when I did it!" He goes away thinking that Westerners have very strange ideas in their heads and are a very mysterious people indeed.

Muslims think that Westerners are unreliable, shifty, full of specious argument, impenetrable, idolatrous in their religion, shameless and without morals. His greatest complaint is that all Westerners look so much alike that you can never tell what they are really thinking. He is much too courteous to say any of this unless pressed to do so after many years of acquaintance and then he will bring forth quite acceptable examples of what he advances. Then one realizes that East is, indeed, East. We have been talking like two men in adjoining sound-proof booths who can see each other through the plate-glass – but each one has been carrying on his own monologue. It is only by actually visiting these lands of Islam that any sort of world-conversation is ever going to be possible.

This first printing of *Living with Islam* is limited to 150 copies.

Also Available from Inkblot:

Stephen Davis
To Marrakech by Aeroplane

Old time Morocco hand Davis returns to the fabled 'red city' of Marrakech after a 7-year absence for a much needed holiday in spring 2008. A delightful account of Marrakech as it embraces the 21st century.

ISBN 0 934301 54 9
$15

Available from:
Aftermath Books
42 Forest St.
Providence, Rhode Island
02906